Reality Bytes

Manageable Bible Meditations for Young People

Julian Hamilton

First published in 1997 by
KEVIN MAYHEW LTD
Rattlesden
Bury St Edmunds
Suffolk IP30 0SZ

0 1 2 3 4 5 6 7 8 9

ISBN 1 84003 069 0
Catalogue No 1500136

Cover illustration by Graham Johnstone
Cover design by Jaquetta Sergeant
Edited by David Gatward
Typesetting by Louise Hill
Printed and bound in Great Britain

Contents

For Mum and Dad

Acknowledgements

There are a number of people who have pushed or helped along the way and I owe them a lot.

Sadie and Sandra for fighting my handwriting and typing the manuscript. Thank you!

Lynda for encouraging me so much to do the project, and David for allowing me to get it done!

No. 22 for giving so much inspiration and wisdom in the whole area of 'life'.

Cheers to those who took the time to read through earlier material and give thoughts and encouragement. You know who you are, so thanks, you made the difference.

Introduction

There is no doubt in my mind that things were an awful lot easier all those years ago when I was a chubby little ten-year-old. Life was simple, home was stable, school was almost fun, and God was God. Over the next ten years God became an increasingly big part of my life; indeed, I would like to think that God has become the meaning of my life.

I am very aware of how good and holy that sounds – if only it was that simple! You see, God has created a wonderful world for us to live, learn and play in, and the more I see of it, the more people I meet, the more life expands, the harder I find it to understand and cope with. Life is an adventure, and there are stories to be written in all of our lives as we travel the paths that we are on. We are all walking along life's road, but we all travel at our own pace, with people going past us, people tripping us up, people helping us through the rocky parts, and others giving us the occasional lift. We all travel as best we can in our own way. *Reality Bytes*, and a second book, *Reality Bytes Again*, have been written to help anyone travelling along those paths honestly and under the guidance of God.

However, they are not 'One Reading a Day' books, so don't get all guilty if you don't read a chapter every day! The passages from the Bible have been arranged to give a little bit of variety. Rather than starting with the Old Testament and finishing with the New Testament, the order is a little more mixed, so don't be surprised if one minute you're listening to Peter, and next hearing about good old Isaiah! And as you zoom around the Bible, take a little time to read around the passage you're looking at; the Bible is a great book and God will speak to you through it; so don't be too surprised if you hear him when you least expect it!

Deeper Than The Skin

GALATIANS 6:7-10

Do not deceive yourselves; no one makes a fool of God. A person will reap exactly what he sows. If he sows in the field of his natural desires, from it he will gather the harvest of death; if he sows in the field of the Spirit, from the Spirit he will gather the harvest of eternal life. So let us not become tired of doing good; for if we do not give up, the time will come when we will reap the harvest. So then, as often as we have the chance, we should do good to everyone, and especially to those who belong to our family in the faith.

It never fails to sadden me the number of people in the world who quietly support violence and suffering. In fact, just about all of us at times can be at fault in this respect. Of course, we would never plant a bomb or pull a trigger but we can still do serious damage.

I went to college with a lot of cool people, but also some dweebs! Some people I met there were nice, some not so nice. Some of them were godly young people and they tried to show God in a positive way as well as living a life they saw as pleasing to him. They sung a lot, prayed a lot, shared their belief in different ways around and outside the college, and generally did good.

One bright afternoon my year had been taking part in EMU activities and no, we weren't running round a zoo chasing big birds that don't fly. Education for Mutual Understanding is part of the government school curriculum to bring Protestant and Catholic pupils and teachers together. It was part of my degree and got me out of lectures for a day! I was chatting with some of my mates on the way back from St Mary's, which is a Roman Catholic teacher training college, when a conversation took place that really disturbed me. Suddenly, my friends turned into narrow-minded, fundamentalist Protestants, sowing seeds of separation.

'Oh, yes, of course we can talk to, be with and pray for our Catholic neighbours, but sharing fellowship, never mind accepting them as equals in God's sight, simply cannot be done!' My heart felt like breaking.

Surely a faith such as ours looks beyond the people, beyond tradition, and goes so much further than doctrinal differences. It is a faith which looks to Christ through the hearts of people and the difference he makes to them. And when we show a spirit of compassion and love to our neighbours, we do what Jesus has commanded us to do again, and again, and again . . .

God,
    I know I restrict you.
I'm sorry.

It's just so easy, Lord,
    not to think about things of which I'm unsure.
So easy to write someone off
    just because they don't agree with me.
But why should they, Lord?

Forgive my impatience,
    my intolerance,
    my mistrust.
Take me to the very heart of the problem,
    and teach me again how to trust,
    respect,
    and cherish the life that you have given to us all.

Use me to show your love in action,
    so that in giving what I can,
    only you know what I may receive.

Keep On Growing

MARK 4:26-29

Jesus went on to say, 'The Kingdom of God is like this. A man scatters seed in his field. He sleeps at night, is up and about during the day, and all the while the seeds are sprouting and growing. Yet he does not know how it happens. The soil itself makes the plants grow and bear fruit; first the tender stalk appears, then the ear, and finally the ear full of corn. When the corn is ripe, the man starts cutting it with his sickle, because harvest time has come.'

Looking at this chapter, do you get the feeling that Mark is trying to tell us something? Three stories about growing, all in the one chapter, and they seem so simple as well (that's always good for me!). I like this one the best. A seed is scattered, the soil makes the seed grow, then with one fell swoop the sickle brings in the harvest – ouch!

What could be more simple?

What I find interesting here (call me bizarre if you want) is what is omitted. I wonder how long the seed took to grow? I wonder how many cold, frosty, middle eastern evenings the young plant struggled through? Let's not forget the fieldmice and other animals that like to nibble on young plants. Not to mention any trimming that needed to be done, like cutting leaves off, or having shoots plucked out by the farmers. It may even have needed a strengthening rod for support. All we know is that the soil made the plant grow and then the harvest came. That's a fairly serious soil!!

We can feel really bad a lot of the time about lots of different kinds of stuff. But let's face it, we are growing. We can feel like giving it all up, and even think (and yes, I've thought it) 'is it all worth it?' But we are still growing. And we won't be fully grown until the harvest comes. And what a harvest! I have a feeling it will be the best thanksgiving ever.

Lord,
    thank you for planting me
    and helping me grow.

Now and again
    I feel sometimes
    that my roots are weak,
    and they don't go deep enough.
My stem is flimsy,
    the wind seems like
    it will knock the stuffing out of me.

But I can feel you, Lord,
    helping me grow.

Slowly,
    steadily,
    continually.

Almost without being noticed,
    the growth goes on.

Make it a good growth, Lord.

Good News

AMOS 8:4-7

Listen to this, you that trample on the needy and try to destroy the poor of the country. You say to yourselves, 'We can hardly wait for the holy days to be over so that we can sell our corn. When will the Sabbath end, so that we can start selling again? Then we can overcharge, use false measures, and tamper with the scales to cheat our customers. We can sell worthless wheat at a high price. We'll find a poor man who can't pay his debts, not even the price of a pair of sandals, and we'll buy him as a slave'. The Lord, the God of Israel, has sworn, 'I will never forget their evil deeds.'

It's not a happy scene, is it? And how about God's words? Hardly the kind of thing that we hear from our pulpits, 'There is going to be mourning and it's going to be serious!'

Mind you, Amos isn't left in any doubt as to why it's going on. God's chosen people neglected the needy. In fact, it's worse than that; they deliberately manipulated the economy so that the poor would stay poor and the people who had, would still have. And they were happy with this system. God obviously wasn't! It's amazing how today so many of our Church leaders' boards, meetings, Church councils, etc., get so agonisingly perplexed about what to do with the world around them. Many of them are genuinely concerned, but oh so many of them (and that includes you and me) are concerned and yet still do nothing. We are just too safe where we are. God takes that very seriously.

The American preacher/writer Jim Wallis tells a story about taking the Bible and cutting out all the bits where the poor and needy are mentioned. He did that, cutting out all the bits where God tells us to take responsibility for those around us. He then took the remaining Bible to church and held it up in front of the congregation. It fell apart.

Our good and great Lord,
Thank you
    for all of your wonderful world.

We are sorry
    for not treating it
    as you would want.

Cheating.
Thinking only of ourselves.
Not looking after the poor.

Show me, Lord,
    what I can do.
It would be great
    to make a difference,
    I'm just not sure I know how.

But I do know
    this world needs your people
    to stand up.

As I stand up, Lord,
    please steady me.

Tripping Down Memory Lane

PROVERBS 2:1-8

Learn what I teach you, my son, and never forget what I tell you to do. Listen to what is wise and try to understand it. Yes, beg for knowledge; plead for insight. Look for it as hard as you would for silver or some hidden treasure. If you do, you will know what it means to fear the Lord and you will succeed in learning about God. It is the Lord who gives wisdom; from him come knowledge and understanding. He provides help and protection for righteous, honest men. He protects those who treat others fairly, and guards those who are devoted to him.

I'm so glad that God is in control. He gives us what we need, and if we don't have something that we think we need, that's because God knows best, thankfully. It is God who gives wisdom, and I for one am glad to try and leave things in his hands.

I spent a weekend with a few of my old school friends a while back. It was over five years since we'd left school (which may not seem like a long time, but wow, it did for us), and we had a lot of talking to do. Of course we'd seen each other since we left, but this was the first time it had been just the four of us, and, as expected, the conversation inevitably came round to the old hall of fame and the question, 'so where are they now?' And my, oh my, there were some surprises. Some of our old school year are married with children, some are doing really well with good jobs and good salaries, whilst others are out of work. There are even some who are dependent on drugs or alcohol. Some have travelled around the world and some haven't even made it out of the parental home! Many are enjoying life, some have found a new life, and a couple have, sadly, lost their lives.

Looking back, there was no way any of us could have foreseen what would happen to the people we came through school with – OK, we could have made a few good guesses (some of them not far off the map), but so much has happened in so little time. God alone gives wisdom. God alone knows why and how. God alone has seen and felt everything all of us have gone through over the last five years, and over the years before. And God alone knows about the next five years, and further, much further.

I get confused sometimes, Lord.
I see the people around me,
    all the good,
    all the bad,
    I even see it in myself.

Questions just flood over me sometimes,
    who?
    why?
    what could I have done?

Lord, please give your peace now,
    to those hurting,
    those in pain,
    those who feel they just can't cope,
    or don't want to.

Also, Lord,
    to those who are fulfilled,
    who are happy,
    who know your love,

give your wisdom.

I'm so glad that you are wisdom
    and knowledge
    and strength.
Can I keep learning from you, Father?

The Proof Is In The Woollies

JUDGES 6:36-40

Then Gideon said to God, 'You say that you have decided to use me to rescue Israel. Well, I am putting some wool on the ground where we thresh the wheat. If in the morning there is dew only on the wool but not on the ground, then I will know that you are going to use me to rescue Israel.' That is exactly what happened. When Gideon got up early the next morning, he squeezed the wool and wrung enough dew out of it to fill a bowl with water. Then Gideon said to God, 'Don't be angry with me; let me speak just once more. Please let me make one more test with the wool. This time let the wool be dry, and the ground be wet.' That night God did that very thing. The next morning the wool was dry, but the ground was wet with dew.

Isn't it comforting to know that the people in the Bible whom we have read and heard stories about since we were tiny children crawling around the living room floor, were just as human as you or I? It's brilliant! We learn the stories (the main ones, that is) and we know them so well, that we think we know all that there is to know about them. Gideon: what a star! Weakest, least listened to, and certainly not someone the Prime Minister would think about for the cabinet! But in the end, possibly the best army general in the world, even though on the way there he was a total chicken!

Imagine testing God: 'OK, Big G, if this really is you talking to me – I mean really you and not just me in my head – if you want me to do this, I mean really want me to do this . . . and I will if you are talking to me, and you do want me to do this . . . then can you just make it a bit easier? I know, I'll stick out this woolly jumper tonight, right? And if this really is you then, urrr, how about making the fleece kind of wet, right, but the ground totally dry? OK? Yeah, that should do it.'

What a toad, scaredy wee wuss! Imagine ever, *ever* talking to

God like that; the cheek of it, the arrogance! Who would ever
think of doing something to ask God to prove himself . . .

God,
   I'm sorry.
I must make it so difficult for you.
I'd love to be able to say 'sometimes'
   at the end of that last sentence,
   but I don't think I can.

It must be really frustrating for you.
Talking to me,
   trying to make me listen,
   and I don't hear you.
And worse,
   I hear what I think you said.

Imagine that, Lord,
   me thinking that I know what you know!

Sorry.

I'd love to be able to hear you clearly, Lord,
   but you dealt with Gideon,
   and just like him,
   I'm scared stiff of what you might say.
Hey, I bet Gideon's face was a picture
   when he saw that fleece!
Did it make you smile, God?
Could I make you smile?
I'll try harder.

As Children

MATTHEW 18:1-5

At that time the disciples came to Jesus, asking, 'Who is the greatest in the Kingdom of Heaven?'

So Jesus called a child, made him stand in front of them, and said, 'I assure you that unless you change and become like children, you will never enter the Kingdom of Heaven. The greatest in the Kingdom of Heaven is the one who humbles himself and becomes like this child. And whoever welcomes in my name one such child as this, welcomes me.'

One of the most significant things in my life to date has been the time spent at Camp Kinawind, in the state of Michigan, America. One particular week a few years ago I was counselling an all-male group. As you can imagine, it was pretty smelly and rude and 'laddish' most of the time, but at other times it was great and we all worked very hard. The group were around the age of twelve and there are a few of them whom I will never forget! One in particular comes to mind. He was rude, ignorant, self-centred and just plain awkward. What a nasty little shock when I read the above verses. OK, so this friend of mine was a bit bigger than the children in the story, but not much. He even caused my most patient co-counsellor and friend to move him to the end of an affirmation line because he needed more time to think of something good to say about him!

God must become saddened by us sometimes. We are his children, and as such have the capacity to think only of ourselves and our needs. Time after time we ask God for things that we don't really need, and I'm sure that all too often we simply turn to God and snap 'no' when he asks us to do things for him. But it doesn't change the fact that we should come to him as his children, humbly and honestly, because after all, he knows best. We may never (on this earth anyway) know all the answers to all the questions, but isn't that what being a child is all about? Being curious, wanting to know the answers, wanting to know and learn continually. Imagine how many times God has heard, 'But why?' . . .

Oddly enough, when I bumped into my young camper friend at a shopping mall in Detroit two weeks later, he introduced me to his mother and told me in front of her that he had enjoyed his best camp experience ever in our group two weeks before. Kids, eh . . . pah!!

Lord, and Father,
   forgive my foolish ways.
Just like one of your little children,
   I huff,
   strop,
   pretend not to hear,
   then cry when I don't get my way.

Wouldn't it be great, Lord,
   if I really could be like a child
   in other ways.

Totally accepting of you
   and who you are.
Totally dependent on you
   and your goodness.
Totally idolising you
   and wanting to be just like 'Dad'.

I want to bounce up and down on your knee,
   I want to know safety in your arms.

Help me, Lord,
   to feel content there,
   and not to jump out
   and run away
   every time I get settled.
Thanks, Lord.

Love Is All You Need

MATTHEW 5:43-48

*'You have heard that it was said, "Love your friends, hate your enemies."
But now I tell you: love your enemies and pray for those who persecute
you, so that you may become the sons of your Father in Heaven. For he
makes his sun to shine on bad and good people alike, and gives rain to
those who do good and to those who do evil. Why should God reward you
if you love only the people who love you? Even the tax collectors do that!
And if you speak only to your friends, have you done anything out of
the ordinary? Even the pagans do that! You must be perfect, just as your
Father in Heaven is perfect!'*

I've always had a little bit of a problem with this one! You see,
loving people who harm others in murderous ways such as
putting bombs under their cars, or shooting them down in front
of family and friends (never mind the more petty scenario of people
I just don't get on with) has never really been a particularly
strong point of mine. I just don't seem to get that certain spark,
and I reckon I'm not altogether alone in that.

But this is interesting. The Greek language had four words for
the one word we would call 'love'. The first is Eros, from which
we get our word 'erotica', so as you can imagine it's a very pas-
sionate, romantic, sexual love. (This word is never used in the
New Testament by the way.) Another word is 'Strage', a love
within the family. The most graphic description here is to note
how many young people, having been abused in some way by a
parent, can often turn round and say something like, 'But she's
still my mother, and I do love her'. The third word for love in the
Greek language is 'Philia' – a love between friends. It's a bonding,
affectionate, respectful and trusting love and can be understood
by anyone who has sat through the night discussing life and the
opposite sex with a friend. But the word used in this instance is

the word 'agape'. This word has been described as 'unconquerable goodwill'. It is not a love we have primarily for family and friends, but is a love that comes from a definite decision to do an action. Christ in the passage above is telling us we need to *do* love. We all need to learn how to do it and then we all need refresher courses as often as we can get them. Christ is our teacher and his spirit our refresher.

We need not be too fond of the people we are loving, but we do need to make the effort to help, encourage, care and be patient with them, and of course, as the passage says, 'pray for them'. It may not be easy (OK, we know it's not easy), but it is God's command. So let's all stop talking about it and *do* it!

Heavenly Father,
You are love.
Perfect, strong.
Uplifting, encouraging.
Forever teaching, and guiding, even me.

Lord, help me to know love,
    your love, so that I can pass it on.
Give it away.

Then, Lord,
    I'll have room for more,
    more of your love,
    and so more of your power.
Thanks, Lord,
    for what that love means for me . . .
Your death.

Thank you, Lord,
    that if I ever need an example
    of love in action, It's you.

Help me keep my eyes on you,
to see your love more clearly.

Nightmares All Around

PSALM 137:1-3

By the rivers of Babylon we sat down;
there we wept when we remembered Zion.
On the willows near by
we hung up our harps.
Those who captured us told us to sing;
they told us to entertain them:
'Sing us a song about Zion!'

The poor Jews; captives in a strange land, and tormented by their oppressors. Probably feeling anxious and unsure about their future as a people. Alone, frightened and remembering Zion, where everything had been so much better.

Those of us under 27 years old and living in Northern Ireland have never, until recently, lived in a 'peaceful land'. Daily coverage of mindless killing, senseless bombing and pointless violence became part of the humdrum of existence. How unfeeling we can become. The Jews in their captivity in a strange land forgot that God was there too. They forgot through all the pain and suffering that God's heart was breaking too. While they cried out to God in anguish for a return to Jerusalem, the seat of the most high, they didn't think that God could have been in their pain with them. They were simply not aware of the compassionate sorrow the Almighty had for them.

How quick we are to complain. How foolish we are when we think God, the Big Guy, has just up and left us and doesn't care any more. We look around in disbelief that God could be here when there is so much pain and hurt going on. We are totally oblivious at times to the fact that he feels all of it. God is a part of our lives, all of our lives. So he loves the laughter and fun and he also holds our heads when we cry. Even when we can't see it.

And something else. The Jews didn't live a few more years and then crash into oblivion at the hands of their captors. Oh no. They were beaten, robbed and badly stung. But they kept the faith and got out of the strange land. From that faith, born of Mary, comes the cornerstone of our faith.

Dear God,
    I suppose that this
    is the most common type of prayer you hear;
'Help me now, I'm sorry.'

I know I've done it,
    and more than once.

It's a fairly amazing thought though, God,
    that you don't ever just clear off.
Thank you for that.

I'm sorry that in those times
    I forget that you know what it's like.
You are there too.

So I suppose
    that I'm saying thank you for that as well,
    for just knowing what it's like
    and for being there too.

Slammin' Rhythms And
Stormin' Bass Lines!

PSALM 150

Praise the Lord!
Praise God in his temple!
Praise his strength in heaven!
Praise him for the mighty things he has done.
Praise his supreme greatness.
Praise him with trumpets.
Praise him with harps and lyres.
Praise him with drums and dancing.
Praise him with harps and flutes.
Praise him with cymbals.
Praise him with loud cymbals.
Praise the Lord, all living creatures!
Praise the Lord!

I have recently been at events where the praise and worship has been hugely encouraging and uplifting. Some of these have even been Methodist organised! Music has the ability to reach the places that words cannot. Sermons, readings, poems and even the most heartfelt and best-scripted messages of encouragement can sometimes fall short. With music there are times when we 'feel' it. As Kingsley said, 'Words speak to our thoughts, but music speaks to our hearts and spirits, to the very core and root of our souls.' I'm not just talking about Christian music. Hothouse Flowers, Seal, Pink Floyd, Genesis, The Wonderstuff, JTQ, Sting, Van Morrison and James Taylor, to name but a few, are artists who at some time – usually more than once – have lifted me up when I've felt down.

With good music in our worship we can travel with the melodies and be touched by the fact that people have been given a talent so helpful to the rest of us. Pianists, guitarists, percussionists, flautists, saxophonists, and even organists! They are special people. Once they are relaxed with their instruments they can feel the music. They can use loud, quiet, fast, slow, powerful (there's bound to be some impressive Italian words for all that!), simple and complicated melodies for the benefit of us all.

If you are one of the above, use your instrument to go deep into the hearts and minds of men, women and children. And if you don't have a good note in your whole body, it doesn't matter! Learn to appreciate the music that finds it's way into your life, and tell the people who make it just how special they are. In that way we will all share in the gift of music.

Father in Heaven, how we love you.
We lift your name over the whole earth.
It's so good, Lord, to feel you close,
    feel like I can touch you,
    know your warmth beside me,
    keeping me safe in your arms.

It's a time when no one,
    not even my own little world
    can butt in
    to destroy a moment of communion.

You have so much for me to learn,
    so much to give,
    in every area of my life.

At times it's the music
    that brings me to you, Lord.
    a helping hand along the way.

Help me to be one of the musicians, Lord,
    with all of my life.

I'm Sorry

JOHN 21:15-17

After they had eaten, Jesus said to Simon Peter, 'Simon son of John, do you love me more than these others do?'
'Yes, Lord,' he answered, 'you know that I love you.'
Jesus said to him, 'Take care of my lambs.' A second time Jesus said to him, 'Simon son of John, do you love me?'
'Yes, Lord,' he answered, 'you know that I love you.'
Jesus said to him, 'Take care of my sheep.' A third time Jesus said, 'Simon son of John, do you love me?'
Peter was sad because Jesus asked him the third time, 'Do you love me?' so he said to him 'Lord, you know everything; you know that I love you!' Jesus said to him, 'Take care of my sheep.'

Peter must have felt terrible. Just think about it: he had spent years listening to and learning from Jesus, telling him that he would rather die than leave him. But remember the 'before the cock crows three times' incident? Peter had let Jesus down, and he knew it. So think how he felt as Jesus kept on asking if he loved him. Was Jesus rubbing it in? Didn't he know how guilty he felt? I don't think that's what Jesus was doing. Perhaps he was just letting Peter know that it's not just about saying sorry, it's about receiving forgiveness and changing.

Here's a little poem of mine about saying sorry.

Is 'sorry' really enough?
Broken hearts, shattered dreams.
A darkening with no apparent sunlight.
Trying to search for adequate words
to express something never felt before.
But can mere words explain and answer?
I think not, for they come not.

Exploring my mind to find the facts,
and when I find them
all I can do is run to hide.
The grim reality of dark desire
ever present holds me there.
But was it done through lack of love?
I think not, for love has gone not.

Telling eyes and knowing smiles,
some aim to comfort,
some aim only to enhance the darkness,
but darkest hour has passed never to return.
Can I be sure, will it happen once more?
I think not. No, I know not.

The dawn is gently seeping through.
Yes.
Shadows beginning to appear
bringing before them glimpses of gold
and earth's finest riches.
Love and friendship, the joy of which are rarely told.
Can I be sure they will not pass?
Yes.

Lord,
    thank you for being forgiving.
Thank you for being loving.

Give me courage.
Courage to know
    when I've really messed up.
Courage to turn into your arms
    when I've been running.

And, Lord,
    help me to find the courage to come back
    when I run for a bit.

What A Mess!

JUDE 1:3-4

My dear friends, I was doing my best to write to you about the salvation we share in common, when I felt the need of writing at once to encourage you to fight on for the faith which once and for all God has given to his people. For some godless people have slipped in unnoticed among us, persons who distort the message about the grace of our God in order to excuse their immoral ways, and who reject Jesus Christ, our only Master and Lord. Long ago the Scriptures predicted the condemnation they have received.

I never thought I'd do it. Never in a million years. In fact I'm so dead against it that I promised myself I couldn't, and simply wouldn't, do it. Now I've just got to.

You see, I've just been watching the news. Upturned vans, burnt-out buses, blockades in the middle of almost every town in the north of Ireland. Thousands of people running around like a swarm of irritable little wasps (spawn of darkness!) pestering, buzzing and stinging wherever they can land.

Once again it unfortunately all began in a church service, probably the only time each year that these people go to church. Then, because they can't dander back home the way they want to, a little bit of hell breaks out. Spurred on and encouraged by – wait for it – churchmen and politicians.

That's it. I've done it. You see, I'm so convinced that creed, colour, or name matters diddly-squat to the Almighty, that I never thought I'd be so cheesed off with 'churchmen' to write something down like 'they are wrong'. But I just did. We've heard it all before. 'Turn the other cheek', 'live and let live', and 'respect each other', but the amount of compassion that I have witnessed on television tonight amounts to something less than the sum of the arguments stating that the Pope is really a Protestant.

I'm all for rights. Believe me, they are vital. They are so close to the heart of God that every time human dignity and need are trampled on, God's heart bleeds. Yet it seems we are still determined to set our own particular set of rights above the needs of others. What never comes into the equation is what Jesus thinks of the whole thing, because all that anyone seems to care about is their own right to walk over someone else's foot, arm, stomach or head. Distorted Christianity?

Almighty, loving,
    and compassionate God,
    what can I say?
Sorry?
And that's just because I happened to be born
    into a particular Church.

Is 'sorry' really enough?
I feel so helpless when people say things like,
    'This is a cause worth dying for'.
I really did hear someone say that, Lord.
Is that the cause you died for?

Maybe I'm just naive,
    too scared to look the situation in the eye.
But I really don't think you're enjoying this.
There are even people on the TV
    with minister collars on.
Why?
What does your peace mean to them?

I suppose I should just keep trying
    to find out what it means to me.
Sorry about all the questions, Lord,
    it's just how I feel.

Simply Not Good Enough?

MATTHEW 10:29-31 AND PSALM 139:1-5

For only a penny you can buy two sparrows, yet not one sparrow falls to the ground without your Father's consent. As for you, even the hairs of your head have all been counted. So do not be afraid; you are worth much more than many sparrows!

Lord, you have examined me, and you know me. You know everything I do; from far away you understand all my thoughts. You see me, whether I am working or resting; you know all my actions. Even before I speak, you already know what I will say. You are all round me on every side; you protect me with your power.

When I think of Christ and his walk on this earth, I have to admit that there are times when it really is too much to take in. Just think of the healing, the teaching. Never has one so wise and powerful walked this earth. The way he treated people, his life of constant prayer, what he said to the priests and ministers; wow! The easiest thing to do sometimes is to dive into my own mind and reconcile myself with the thought of being totally inadequate. I'm simply not good enough.

Take for example my good old college 'mucho party' days. Just about every textbook sin that I heard about at school and church was covered and then doubled for good measure and experience. Boy, did I learn. I went to Stranmillis College, Belfast (not a place with the height of rebellious tendencies!) There was a large Christian population and to set the scene, when I meet some of my past student buddies and tell them what I'm doing now, I have to pick them up off the floor. However, I don't live in regret or guilt. I realised a while ago that if I waited until I felt good and worthy enough to work for the Church I would be waiting for a very, very, very, long time. God uses us the way we are, shabby

though we may be. I know his love for me and I know that he
demands I pass it on. I don't get it right all the time, indeed I get
it wrong most of the time, but to think that I'm rubbish is to insult
God. He made me. He loves me and when I'm in tune enough he
still uses me in ways he sees fit. Now that's what I call a miracle!

My God,
   who is loving and whose mercy overflows,
   take me, and use me.

You know how I can get, Lord;
   frustrated, feeling weak,
   angry,
   wondering if I can make the grade.

Father, watch me
   with those loving eyes,
   search me,
   so I can know myself.

Take the good,
   take the bad,
   take it all, Lord
   so I can have it back.
Renewed,
   mended,
   up to scratch.

Oh . . . and Father,
   the next time I feel I'm no good,
   or I've nothing to say . . .
Hold me, Lord,
In your hands.
So that I can't run away.

Don't Panic!

JOSHUA 1:6-7, 9

Be determined and confident, for you will be the leader of these people as they occupy this land which I promised their ancestors. Just be determined, be confident; and make sure that you obey the whole Law that my servant Moses gave you. Do not neglect any part of it and you will succeed wherever you go. . . . Remember that I have commanded you to be determined and confident! Don't be afraid or discouraged, for I, the Lord your God, am with you wherever you go.

Here was Joshua; Moses had been the great leader of the people for years, and now it was his turn. Scared? I think so! If you look at the first five verses you'll read about the promises, the directions, the results of what the Lord is going to do. And it's simple; they, the Israelites, are going to have it all. God tells them.

But there's more. Even after the promises and the confirmation of God's action plan, in the next four verses God still has to go on building up his people, telling them not to panic, because he is going to be with them. Sounds familiar, doesn't it? It's almost a 'Go on and don't worry, it's going to be OK!'

How many times do we panic about what God's plan is for us? Going on a two-week mission over the summer perhaps, leading a prayer meeting (which of course as we all know means that you have to pray first!), playing the guitar in Youth Fellowship, or even worse in Church! It may not be as dramatic as the plans that God had for the Israelites, but he still has plans for us. The difficult bit for us is the obedience – not easy. It's worth remembering that these plans from the Lord for the Israelites came after a lot of heartbreak for God by their disbelief (check out the golden bull), yet still the love shows itself through trusting them for their future. They failed before and they would fail later, but God still worked with them and loved them.

Seems funny, but obedience to God breeds more obedience

because when we feel his touch and see the guiding light, and know the strength that simply isn't anything like us, then who can resist wanting more? Yes, we mess up, yes, we try to run away sometimes, but not only will God continue in his plans for us, he will forget the past to concentrate on the future. Who knows which future diplomat, rock star, prime minister, or writer may look back to these verses for strength. I know I do already.

Dear God,
    I've got to admit,
    I know you know best.

And thank you
    for keeping on trying to tell me
    what it is.

Sorry I don't catch on
    as quick as I should.

I'm going to take a bit of time now, God,
    would you like to chat about some ideas?

Just Being Nosey

ECCLESIASTES 11:9-10

Young people, enjoy your youth. Be happy while you are still young. Do what you want to do, and follow your heart's desire. But remember that God is going to judge you for whatever you do. Don't let anything worry you or cause you pain. You aren't going to be young very long.

It was a beautiful evening in early June, and the last traces of the sunset across Belfast Lough were lengthening the shadows and darkening the corners in Groomsport. I was sitting in my car waiting for a friend and was getting ready to drive home. In the bus shelter beside where I was parked there was a group of about eight young people aged about thirteen to seventeen years, and what an interesting conversation I was able to 'leech-in' on.

They were talking about religion. God, creation, the Bible, humanity, the Church, etc. The beer they had already downed probably made discussion slightly easier, and more than likely added to the honesty! What really hit me was the sincerity with which most of them spoke. Obviously God was someone who was real to them. Not real in the sense of a unique creator being who gave them life for which they were eternally grateful, but nonetheless a reality. Two of them insisted on the truth of the Bible and wouldn't let the others convince them of anything else. They were ordinary young people, just like you and me. There was one boy who stood out in the discussion and it seemed like he had more knowledge of biblical things than a lot of us. But he had a problem. To use his words he enjoyed 'the good life'. He held nothing against the Church, nothing against God, but he couldn't accept Christianity because, as he perceived it, this would mean a change in his life to what he saw as the accepted 'normal Christian', and he simply didn't want that.

I find that really sad in two ways. Firstly, he didn't want to be a Christian because of the Christians he had seen. That's us he is looking at. And secondly he's totally missed the mark. He was intelligent and he knew the Bible, but he didn't understand that Jesus calls us to him. Not to a church or a denomination, but to him and his service. If only they had discussed the one person in the Bible that may have helped them make sense of it. If only they had known that Jesus doesn't look on us the way we look on each other. If only I'd had the courage to get out of the car.

Lord,
    it's sad sometimes, to see
    what we have done to your way.

You call,
    and we turn away.
You call,
    and *we* say what *you* mean.
You call,
    and we simply can't hear,
    or won't.

Yet when I think about it,
    it could be no other way.
You are perfect, and I'm not.

Thanks, Father, for loving me
    even to the extent
    of repeating what you said
    because I didn't listen.

Thanks that you love us all as we are,
    no strings attached.
Thanks that you alone hold the answers.
Not a single church,
    not a denomination,
    not even our favourite minister or leader,
    but you alone; the Lord God Almighty.

You're Gorgeous!

GENESIS 1 AND 2:1-2

. . . By the seventh day God finished what he had been doing and stopped working.

What a big chunk of Bible! It's also an amazing one. To think that God made the world that we live in. Wow! Even more remarkable is that in verses 29-30 it is then given to you and me to look after – and aren't we doing a good job. NOT.

There was a time (not too long ago) when I was quite into looking at different theories of creation. You know, God versus science and all that stuff. Cosmology is a seriously big topic, way too big for a little guy like me. What happened in the end of this star search was simple. I asked myself, 'who cares?' What matters to me is that God made it – do I really think I'm ever going to understand how he did it? Wise up. This is the God who made the universe and it's really big! So how can anyone expect to answer satisfactorily how he made this planet – never mind how he made us?

My favourite bit in the above story is this: 'And God was pleased with what he saw.' Again and again the Almighty looked and liked it – wouldn't you?

I wish I could take you to the Canoe Boundary Waters Wilderness in the state of Minnesota, USA. It's an amazing place and I was lucky enough to be there a couple of years ago. No houses, no roads, no power boats, just thousands of miles of lakes and rivers. As I canoed around a small part of the vast wilderness with a group of about fifteen others, God touched me. I watched the eagles fly across the setting sun, I heard other birds calling to each other to mark the threat, I heard the wolves howl in the darkness and I got bitten by hundreds of mosquitoes, and it was beautiful!

Why not go and look wherever you can to see the beauty of

this world. The purity, the care, the wonder. What a wonderfully creative and imaginative God we have and he is still making things new, including us. It's amazing that you will never have to look too far for a wonder of creation because at this moment God could be pointing at you, nudging St Peter and saying, 'Isn't he/she marvellous. Just beautiful.'

What a world, Lord.
It's brilliant,
    so innovative.
Right from us,
    to creepy crawly things,
    you did it all,
    even a duck-billed platypus.
Amazing!

Thank you for the responsibility, Lord,
    that comes with being human;
    having to look after this world.
We are so bad at it though, Lord.
I'm sorry.

I want to be better at it, Lord,
    I'd really like to see your creating hand everywhere.
To see how you made it,
    and why.
But that's impossible because you made it
    and I didn't.
Thanks for letting me be a part of it.

What Do You Mean, Impatient?!

JAMES 5:7-8

Be patient, then, my brothers, until the Lord comes. See how patient a farmer is as he waits for his land to produce precious crops. He waits patiently for the autumn and spring rains. You also must be patient. Keep your hopes high, for the day of the Lord's coming is near.

Strange couple of verses, eh? Mind you, a lot of God's word seems strange to me! So often I appeal to God like a little child, climbing on to his knee, saying, 'But why? But why? But why?'

And so on those grounds I can say that the picture of a farmer waiting patiently for crops to grow isn't a picture that I can readily jump up and down to and exclaim, 'Yes, I've got it!' The reason being that any farmers I have met, and I've met a few, certainly aren't a picture of tranquillity and rest. They are amongst some of the busiest and hardest working men and women that I have ever met. Up out of bed so early that it scares me (it's a concept that I can't seem to get a hold of), out in the fields, round with the tractor, buying and selling livestock at the mart, preparing the ground, etc. Always trying to plan ahead and be ready for all the things that weather or anything else may bring. And, boy, are they protective of their land and livestock!

But maybe that's right. Maybe patience shouldn't be something that is on the surface, but should be something deep down. A resistance to fickleness and foolishness. A rooted trust in an eventuality. A state of heart that means you work all the harder due to contentment of the mind.

But hang on; the farmers I've met are always complaining! Perhaps that's because there's always something to be done? Now there's a thought.

Lord, God,
   you give peace,
   you give serenity,
   you give calmness of heart and mind,
   you give a real patience.

Sorry, Lord, for those silly times.

You know,
   the ones when I whined at you and said,
   'No. I want it *now*!'

I suppose patience
   isn't just something that's nice to have,
   it's a way of life.
The way you are.

Thank you for being
   so patient with me, Lord.

I'll Stand By You

MATTHEW 25:45

... 'I tell you, whenever you refused to help one of these least important ones, you refused to help me.'

Jesus takes it straight to the heart; hunger, poverty, illness, loneliness, depression – that's where the work is. That is where Jesus wants us to be. That is where we should be working. Think about this:

I am homeless.
I have no bed and no pillow to put my head on.
I can't get any easy food to eat.
No Sunday lunch for me this week at my parents' house,
(and they haven't tried to find me since I left).
And yes, I'm angry at God.

I'm sick.
I've been housebound for two and a half years.
Outside my family, only seven people have bothered to visit.
My wife has to work harder now; she keeps us both.
And yes, I'm angry at God.

I'm alone.
My husband left me five months ago;
ran off with a tart.
Got to pay the mortgage myself.
Got no other family.
No friends.
I went to church once or twice after it happened.
No one talked to me.
So yes, I'm angry at God.

Everyone feels alone, or scared, or left out at some point in their life. Do you know where you are? What pain are you keeping to yourself because you think God doesn't understand?

I'm hungry and dirty.
I'm frustrated and helpless.
I'm alone and scared.

Why not just be honest with God? He loves you, he knows what you're going through, and he does understand.

I feel ashamed and worthless.
I feel ugly and burdensome.
I feel rejected and horrible.

No matter how you feel, God feels this pain with you. Tell him! Yell it out and cry to God about how you feel, and why.

Lord,
I'm desperate to hear your voice.
To know that you are here with me,
in this darkness.

I am crushed by my thoughts,
held down by my anger
and chained by my tears.

I can do nothing
except cry out to you,
my God.

Hear me, Lord.

See For Yourself

GALATIANS 6:7

Do not deceive yourselves; no one makes a fool of God. A person will reap exactly what he sows.

I was looking through a Bible in my house the other day, as you do, when I saw something a bit strange. Verse 7 of Galatians chapter 6 was highlighted and as far as I could see, there wasn't another highlighted passage to be found. This being the case, my mind began to wonder 'why'? 'what'? and 'when'? It is one of my Dad's Bibles, so rather than ask him, I left it to my own imagination as to what he was thinking whenever it was he read and highlighted it. My mind flirted with several possibilities as to reasons for this, some of them probably fairly plausible, when it struck me that the important thing to do was to ask what this verse said to me. It was then that the verse really began to challenge me.

After all that, I'm not going to write here and now what that verse did say to me as I sat in my Dad's study that day. That would defeat the purpose of what it taught me. You see, I learned that people have to read the Bible for themselves; you have to let God's spirit speak to you in ways that you can understand. I'm sure that there are people who get something completely different out of the verse above, but I'm also sure that if they are trusting in God to speak to them and they have a heart ready to listen, then who am I to tell them they are wrong because a verse said something different to me than it did to them? God is bigger than us, all of us, and he speaks to us in different ways all the time. Most important is the fact that if I get a chance to hear what God says to you through the above piece of scripture, I should listen.

Father Almighty,
    your word is powerful.
You call it a sword.
Cutting,
    getting through the most hardened areas
    of human life.

Lord, help me to use it more,
    be better at swordsmanship,
    able to cut finely and skilfully
    at areas of danger and hurt.

You see, Lord,
    most of the time I use it badly.
Like a limp baton,
    not a powerful weapon.
I'm sorry, Lord.

Renew your spirit in me, Lord,
    make me a real spiritual soldier,
    with a wondrous weapon,
    that I know how to use.

Your words,
    your life,
    your death for me,
    your plan for us all.
Thank you for it, Lord.

Every Second Counts

ROMANS 8:28

We know that in all things God works for good with those who love him, those whom he has called according to his purpose.

I used to think that I understood all the good things that Paul writes about. I knew what I needed, I knew what I had and didn't have, and I knew what I longed for. I never seemed to think that God was working for the good in my life, and that in the end all the bad things may just serve a purpose for tomorrow. Here's a poem by a lesser known poet (that's me, by the way!) that says to hang on to all that we go through. Because that is what shapes us. And God works it all.

He ran a bit of a marathon once,
    doesn't think he could do it now.
He drummed in rock bands once or twice,
    doesn't think he could do it now.

He used to think he could do anything,
    doesn't think that any more.
He used to want only to be thin,
    doesn't think that any more.

He used to want everything to be perfect,
    doesn't think it ever will be.
He used to ask girls out for a date,
    doesn't think that will ever be.

I hope to God he looks up soon,
    'cos all he can see now is murky gloom.
Just remember, all that's gone, with more to come
    shapes the man.
That's you my son.

Dear God,
    I know I can forget really easily
    that you are working
    with all that I go through.

I'm really quick to forget
    that you work for good.

I get scared,
    anxious
    and frustrated,
    and plain angry,
    just because I think
    I'm the one in control.

Thank you for reminding me that I'm not.

Don't let me forget.

This Little Light Of Mine

JOHN 8:12

Jesus spoke to the Pharisees again. 'I am the light of the world,' he said. 'Whoever follows me will have the light of life and will never walk in darkness.'

I love doing this type of thing, you know, using candles and things. Let me explain. A few years ago at a camp in America where I worked for a while, I was what they call a 'dean' for the week, which means it was kind of my camp for the week! Cool! At the end of every week there we had a celebration, which consisted of singing, dancing, listening, praying and usually communion. On this occasion I gave every camper (about sixty of them) a candle. We were in a clearing in the forest, totally surrounded by trees and woodland. It was dark except for the light from the campfire (that I had built and which was going rather well if I do say so myself) and the stars were spread across the sky above us.

It was a very special night. We told each other stories of our week and we shared Communion together. Then, one person lit a candle from the fire and began to pass the flame around the circle. Slowly the darkness was pushed away as more candles were lit. Once the light had passed round all of us, it was amazing! Every camper held a 'light', a little bit of flame which they were invited to keep alight for as long as possible and then remember that Jesus, as light of the world, gives them light in their lives.

To finish the evening, they walked back to their cabins using the light from their candles. There were no torches turned on, so all I could see was a line of little lights going through the dark forest and disappearing through the trees. The light they had shone in front of them showing the way, but the light they had inside was of even more importance. It is a light to guide us through life.

Lord,
    light is such a cool thing.
It shows us the way through darkness,
    points out things we may not have seen.

I know there are times
    when it's been too dark for me.
I get scared,
    wondering what is in the shadows,
    wondering where you are.

Forgive me, Father,
    for not asking you to guide me.
The times when you are lighting a perfectly safe way
    and I stumble towards the darker place.

Let your light shine on,
    let it shine in me and through me,
    showing up darkness around me,
    and within me.

Guide me, Lord,
    in your light.

Surprise, Surprise!

LEVITICUS 22:3

If any of your descendants, while he is ritually unclean, comes near the sacred offerings which the people of Israel have dedicated to me, he can never again serve at the altar. This applies for all time to come. I am the Lord.

I really surprised myself a little while earlier on today. Here's how ... I sat down and flicked through the book of Leviticus! Not the type of thing that working young people (and I *am* still a young person at the age of twenty-four) usually do on a morning away from the office! But let me tell you, this Bible we have is just full of surprises. Did you know, for example, that as well as having to be ritually 'clean' all the time – which by the way, from what I have read seems to be exceedingly difficult – there are a few more hidden surprises? Here are a couple of choice spiritual cuts:

If a man marries both a woman and her mother, they have to be burned in fire.
If a man sleeps with his aunt, they will both die childless.
Priests must not shave their heads or cut off the edges of their beards and they cannot marry a prostitute either.
Do not do anything that endangers your neighbour's life.
Do not eat any meat with blood still in it.
Do not mate two different kinds of animals or plant two crops in the same field.
Do not wear clothing woven of two types of material.

There are even directions on rashes, medical discharge, periods, childbirth and mildew – I kid you not! So what's this got to do with me? Hmmmm.

To be honest, I'm not totally sure that I have a good answer. What I can see is that most of the 'laws' are brilliant for the Israelites who live in a community in the desert. It seems to be about keeping health and sanity under a supreme God. It also talks about not cheating, lying, slandering, being greedy, etc., and that has to be a good thing. Then there is Jesus. Remember how the Pharisees were always on at him for breaking these laws? What Jesus said has to be our first consideration: 'Love God and love your neighbour.' And if you can get those two things totally sussed, then go ahead and begin to work with all the others.

Dear Lord,
    your Bible is a really cool book.
Thank you for it – again!
There's so much to take in and think about,
    and I'm not sure I'm very good at doing that.

I know it's the best thing to do,
    to get into it,
    really know it.
I pray, Lord,
    for a heart to capture what it is saying to me.
To pick out the things
    you want to make a difference to my life.

Big things.
Little things.
Whatever they are.

May I read your book to aid my life.
It's such a wonderful gift, Lord.
Help me to make full use of it.

Reality Bites

JONAH 4:1-3

Jonah was very unhappy about this and became angry. So he prayed, 'Lord, didn't I say before I left home that this is just what you would do? That's why I did my best to run away to Spain! I knew that you are a loving and merciful God, always patient, always kind, and always ready to change your mind and not punish. Now, Lord, let me die. I am better off dead than alive.'

It would'nt be unfair to read the above passage and think of Jonah being an 'ungrateful wee pig!' but that would not be nice. Think over the story. God tells Jonah to go to Nineveh. Jonah decides that Spain is much nicer. Jonah becomes fishbait. God uses Jonah to do his good works in Ninevah. Jonah looks and thinks, 'Well that worked, not!' (paraphrased, of course). After all that had happened and all the good God has used him to do, Jonah, at the end of it all, is still being surprised that God keeps his word and does what he says he will do. That's not too far away from many Christians today.

Part of what I do in 'real life' is to help organise and take part in youth events. Sometimes, whenever a lot of prayer is put into an event, together with hard work and preparation by a good team, God really touches people. When this happens there are sometimes those of us who are still a little surprised by it! That's pretty sad, isn't it? What I hear people saying after God has touched them is that the whole event and experience was wonderful, but it's now time to get back to their own church. Reality bites; ouch! It always makes me really sad.

There are no quaint easy answers, although I do think that a serious attempt to address the issue goes a long way in dealing with it. Many people simply refuse to accept that things need to change. I do know that as a Church of God, and as a people of

God, if we are going to pray for his Spirit to move and his will to be done, then we have to open ourselves to what that means. Many of us probably don't know what we are really asking for when we pray for more of God to surround us. It's a dangerous business, this prayer thing. After all, God's listening!

Loving Father God,
   you are all there is
   that really matters.
You know all the questions,
   you have all the answers.
You are so much more
   than I can ever imagine,
   and I almost shake at what I am about to pray
   but I'll pray it anyway.

Surprise me, Lord.
   I ask for your power in my life
   in my church,
   in my town,
   in my country.

And I pray that I can believe in what you can do
   and not be so surprised when you do it.
I'm looking forward to seeing you in action.

Transformed

ACTS 2:14

Then Peter stood up with the other eleven apostles and in a loud voice began to speak to the crowd: 'Fellow-Jews and all of you who live in Jerusalem, listen to me and let me tell you what this means.'

It was about ten years ago and I was with twenty-five other people. We were camping in a forest somewhere in Germany (don't ask me where, forests in Germany all seem to look the same to me!) and we were having a great time, but here's the catch. We didn't know when it would happen, but we knew that one night, some guys from the local village would sneak through the forest, and try to steal the flag on our flagpole. So, every night we had two watches, from 12 midnight to 1 am and from 1 am to 2 am. Now believe me, the night I did the second watch with one other guy from Ireland was a very scary experience. Just a load of tents, a load of trees and many shadows. There was one point when an owl decided to sing for us. Having lived most of my life up to this point in large towns in Northern Ireland where I had never heard a 'twit-twoo', this gave me a considerable fright. In fact, I had great trouble keeping my pants dry. I was convinced it was the Germans! But it wasn't.

Later in the week, when I wasn't on duty (thankfully), they came. We were woken up by bangers going off and people running around, shouting. Then it happened. I got an extra dose of adrenaline! Boy, did I get a rush. I chased after two of them down the main track through the forest and as they got away, I turned to see three more coming straight at me. I took my mark, started for them and did what I think is possibly the best rugby tackle I have ever done in my entire life! (Ask the people I played rugby with, there weren't very many tackles from me!) The poor bloke I caught was flattened! Help arrived and we took him back to camp. The funny thing is, next day at breakfast, the other Irish guys who had seen the whole thing happen told everybody about it! I was a hero for an hour or two. Talk about a transformation. Feeble guy who nearly wet his pants at the sound of an owl, to fearless raging defender of the flag!

That's exactly what took place in the passage above. Previous to this, Peter had messed up big time. He had lied, hidden and tried to run from Jesus at different times. What a transformation! A transformation only God could help him make. The best bit – it can happen to us as well.

Father, I really want to thank you.
I think it's great that there are stories in the Bible
   which have good endings!

It must have been hard
   to watch Peter run away,
   then deny he had even known you.
But it's a great transformation,
   a real turn around.

Standing up in front of people,
   telling them about you
   and letting your Spirit work.
I pray, Lord,
   that I will do the same.
That I will learn how to look for you,
   learn how to let your Spirit work through me,
   and learn how to let you transform my life.

Please do it, Lord,
   here's my life,
   turn it around.

Party Time!

DEUTERONOMY 14:28-29

At the end of every third year bring the tithe of all your crops and store it in your towns. This food is for the Levites, since they own no property, and for the foreigners, orphans, and widows who live in your towns. They are to come and get all they need. Do this and the Lord your God will bless you in everything you do.

I will always remember many of the places of worship I have been in. Unfortunately, some of the reasons are not that good. Here are some things which I recall:

- Having to talk from a pulpit (to do otherwise would be unthinkable)
- Not being able to hold a worship service in a church hall
- Humour *was not* appropriate in worship
- The church where young people were *not* allowed to hold a dance. (King David did that by the way. Check out 1 Chronicles, 15)
- The church officials reprimanding a congregation because its monetary 'giving' was pathetic.

This money business is of great interest to me, especially since so many churches tend to put a huge emphasis on this. I find the above passage in Deuteronomy astounding; I've never heard a sermon about it. A tenth of all that God's people had was to be set aside, and every third year it was set aside for the poor and needy (known as a 'tithe'). The other years (read vs. 22-26) it was set aside for a party! Now that's what I like! The people of Israel were told by God to look after the poor and needy, there is no question of that, but a tithe was only used for that every third year. Although much was done for the poor, God still wanted his people to party. To eat, drink, dance, be happy and enjoy what he had given them. Just how amazing is that? So party on; God says so!

Heavenly Lord,
    thank you for being a wonderful God.

A party!
The idea just cracks me up!

I can just imagine
    telling my minister
    that we have to save for a big party!

I'm sorry that as your people
    we miss out on so much
    of what you want to do for us.
You want us to enjoy being your people.
Live life to the full,
    experience real joy
    and have a party.

I want to thank you
    for being real to me
    and talking in words I understand.
Praise your name, Lord.

Wind Your Neck In!

2 PETER 3:8-9

'But do not forget one thing, my dear friends! There is no difference in the Lord's sight between one day and a thousand years; to him the two are the same. The Lord is not slow to do what he has promised, as some think. Instead he is patient with you, because he does not want anyone to be destroyed, but wants all to turn away from their sins.'

Sometimes there are things in life that come along and irritate us. When they come to me I really don't seem to be that good at dealing with them. You probably know what I mean. The things/people/places/circumstances that make you say the rudest thing you know at the top of your voice! (If you never do this, then you are a very nice person; keep it up!)

I had a day a while ago when everything went wrong. It had all started a week before, with my car failing an MOT test due to an oil leak. The fact that the car had been at the garage before the test that same day made this even more frustrating. So now I had to take the car back again.

Having left the car at the garage for the morning to fix the leak I remember that the tax and insurance documents which I need for the test are in my parents' house about twenty miles away! Having phoned my dad to hunt out the documents for me to collect on my way from the garage to the test centre, I arrive at the garage to discover that they haven't fixed the oil leak! I am not happy as the test is only two hours away. I now phone Dad to beg him to meet me at the test centre with the documents, but unfortunately Mum has the car and he doesn't know when she'll be back!

At last the car is ready and I eventually arrive at the test centre minus the documents and five minutes late. I manage to persuade the two mechanics to look at the car which they do and at last the certificate is signed.

Don't you just hate it when something small goes crazy, the pressure builds and soon your life looks like it may well be ruined? Do you think Jesus ever got stressed out over time? Thank goodness that God is outside time. It is nothing to him; he is above/beyond/around and over it. That's not just brilliant and inspiring (God's good at both of those), it's very comforting too.

I really let it get to me sometimes, Lord.
It takes over.

'I've no time.'
'There's too little time.'
'I'll see what the time is.'

It's so easy to get caught up in, Lord,
    that I forget that you have given me this time,
    and you want me to use it the best way possible.
Which I think means you want me to be
    happy and fulfilled in it.
And that's when I get stressed about it, Lord.

So, Lord,
    when the hands on the clock are racing
    and time is overtaking me,
    help me to stop,
    relax a little,
    and give you a little of the time
    you have given to me.

In Your Face

2 PETER 1:16

We have not depended on made-up stories in making known to you the mighty coming of our Lord Jesus Christ. With our own eyes we saw his greatness.

'Well, they got it easy . . .'

If you are in any way human, you will at one time or another have muttered something like, 'They were lucky; they got to see him and that makes it so much easier.' And of course it would be. So much scepticism, so much thinking time and so much doubt could be cut out of the whole picture of Christianity if we could just see the physical Jesus and have a chat. I'm jealous of those early disciples and followers.

I've seen all the sketches and plays. The ones that end with the highly dramatic clinching ending that goes something like, 'Oh, and one more thing about Jesus. I know he's real, 'cos I've met him.' Let's face it; delivered with conviction, this can be a very powerful ending. But I do have to say that on a couple of occasions I have been left thinking (like the biggest heretic in the world), 'Now excuse me, but *how*?' It makes me feel guilty, but I can't help thinking that it would be so much easier with a physical sign now and again.

Then again, it didn't stop Peter from pretending he never knew Jesus. Come to think of it, it didn't prevent Judas deciding on the money instead. Then there was the rich young ruler who just turned and walked away, and what about all those Pharisees?!

Maybe the whole thing has got something to do with only seeing what we want to, rather than searching for what is really there. We take such a great leap of faith if we do actually search for Jesus in this world. He comes to us in the hungry, the poor, the desperate, the lonely, and in so many other ways. I dread to think

how many times I look into the face of Jesus and don't recognise
him. Perhaps I should look a little harder?

Jesus, my Lord,
   I know I would have loved
   to watch you in action;

    laughing,
    crying,
    teaching,
    healing,
    being with people.

I think that's what you did best.
You simply 'were'
   with people.

Your friends must have felt so lucky
   to be beside you.

My problem, Lord,
   is that I think it should be different now
   because I can't physically see you.

But really, you are here, Lord.
Through your people.
Through me.

Help me be more like you, Lord.

Tight Squeezes

MARK 10:47-50

When he heard that it was Jesus of Nazareth, he began to shout, 'Jesus! Son of David! Take pity on me!' Many of the people scolded him and told him to be quiet. But he shouted even more loudly, 'Son of David, take pity on me!' Jesus stopped and said, 'Call him'. So they called the blind man. 'Cheer up!' they said. 'Get up, he is calling you.' He threw off his cloak, jumped up, and came to Jesus.

I remember standing amongst several thousand people at Greenbelt a few years ago watching Brian Kennedy live on 'main stage'. (Absolutely brilliant by the way. If you ever get the chance, go see him; a great guy, a top musician, and a good Irish man!) I was having a 'toptastic time'. When Brian finished there was one more act to come that night. Moby. Pretty darn good if you're into that kinda stuff. I'm not. Well, each to his own and all, just not exactly my cup of tea. Anyway, there I was, very close to the front, Brian gone, Moby coming, when it happened.

Unknown to me (because I hadn't been looking very hard) a load of hard-core Moby fans had closed in. Tons of them, serious ravers! So, whenever Moby came bouncing on (as he does) and the music started, I was caught in what can only be described as giant waves of dance. I was getting tired, I was beginning to sweat like a pig, and I couldn't really go anywhere. Argh! Who says purgatory isn't real? I was being bounced against my will!

Funny, but Jesus must have caused stirs like that quite often. Again and again we read about crowds gathering round him, or travelling to see him, or following him. It must have gotten quite tight. Try and picture this. A blind man hears the commotion, and asks what on earth is happening. Someone tells him (or he just hears) that it is Jesus, who he has heard about already. The crowd jostle and push around him trying to get close to Jesus, and what happens? Jesus stops and says to someone, 'call him'. Amazing, and people think the only miracle here was giving the man back his sight. Imagine being the blind man, in the middle of clamouring, shouting, pushing and perhaps outright arrogant people. Jesus calls you and brings you out, brings you to safety, brings you to yourself. Then he heals you. Wow!

Jesus,
    I love the way you did things.
Shocked people,
    amazed them.
Made some angry,
    some happy.

I thank you
    that this story reminds me
    of what is important.
Because there is so much
    pushing and shoving in life,
    that I get caught up in it.

But you can take me
    by the hands
    and bring me out.

Take me by the hand to a quiet place.

What Do You Want To Do?

AMOS 3:8

When a lion roars, who can avoid being afraid? When the Sovereign Lord speaks, who can avoid proclaiming his message?

I don't like to admit this, but I've always been rather envious of those people who know exactly what they want to do with their lives. You know the ones; those at school who chose the right GCSEs, the right A levels, the right degree and went straight into the job they'd always wanted. I have never really been able to understand this because I have never felt like this. Even now, enjoying what I do, I'm not sure it's what I really want to do. I felt like this at college, at school, all through my life, in fact! One thought that has crossed my mind more than anything, is what it would be like to be called by God to do a specific job. No questions asked, this is it. No questioning, confusion, indecision or worry. Nice and simple; do it because God says so!

Amos was called to be a prophet. He probably didn't want to be one because he was happy being an agriculturist. But when God said 'prophesy', he did it. And it got him into a lot of trouble. Read some of his book sometime, he really does say some things that made him very unpopular. He certainly wouldn't be invited to many after-dinner functions!

It was the same with other prophets too. Many of them experienced real heartache, struggle and isolation. Why? Because God told them to prophesy, so what else could they do?

We need prophets today. People who will challenge the normal. Remind the Church about obligations to the poor, talk about injustice openly and freely, and not get upset because they have made people feel uncomfortable. Christianity is uncomfortable. It should never become cushy or relaxed. So if you have something to say because God is telling you to say it – say it; the world needs it.

Lord God,
   almighty maker and amazing friend.
If you have something for me to say,
   please give me the courage to say it.
I suppose it's a bit silly asking that,
   because I know you have things for me to say.
So, really I'm asking you to forgive me
   for not saying it already.
And I'm saying I will try and be a better listener!
I know your people should be dangerous,
   and I know we act a bit like pussy cats
   instead of lions.
But help me to speak your words,
   or at least encourage and spread the words of people
   you have appointed to do that.

Thank you.

Sources